Animal Facts Cursive Handwriting Workbook for Kids

Animal Facts

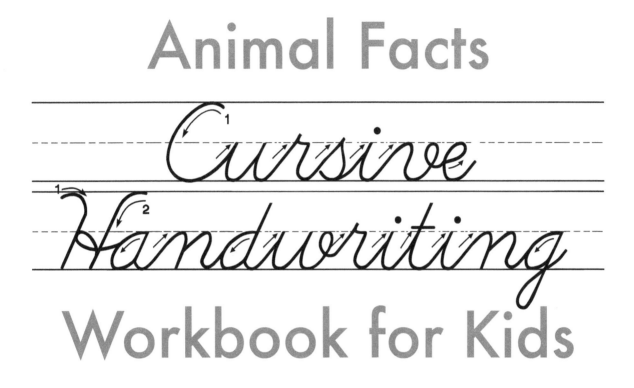

Cursive Handwriting

Workbook for Kids

Learn and Practice the Alphabet
with Animal Words and Sentences!

Crystal Radke

ROCKRIDGE
PRESS

This book is dedicated to my parents, Michael and Judy, and my sister, Lindsay, for supporting my love for learning and always encouraging me to follow my heart.

First Rockridge Press trade paperback edition 2022

Rockridge Press and the Rockridge Press logo are trademarks or registered trademarks of Callisto Media Inc. and/or its affiliates in the United States and other countries and may not be used without written permission.

For general information on our other products and services, please contact our Customer Care Department within the United States at (866) 744-2665, or outside the United States at (510) 253-0500.

Paperback ISBN: 978-1-68539-431-8

Manufactured in the United States of America

Interior and Cover Designer: Mando Daniel and Irene Vandervoort
Art Producer: Maya Melenchuk and Sue Bischofberger
Editor: Annie Choi
Production Editor: Ruth Sakata Corley
Production Manager: Lanore Coloprisco

All illustrations used under license from Shutterstock, iStock, and 123RF
Author photo courtesy of Twenty Toes Photography

10 9 8 7 6 5 4 3 2 1 0

Note to Parents

In a time of increased technology use, it is important that we continue to have children practice handwriting regularly to help with their cognitive development. Cursive handwriting activates a different part of the brain than typing. This stimulation helps children develop early reading skills. This book will be perfect for learners ages seven to ten. Not only will they learn how to write in cursive, but they will also gain so much knowledge about animals.

These handwriting pages were designed to support your young learner by making it fun and engaging. Coloring sheets will provide a great brain break with additional fine motor practice, too. Be sure to compare your child's handwriting before and after by using the page provided.

By working through this book, your child will:

- Strengthen their fine motor skills

- Increase their kinesthetic memory as they work on handwriting patterns

- Increase the development of visual and motor parts of their brain

To help your child be successful, we have formatted this book in sections. First, they will practice each letter, starting with capital letters and then progressing to lowercase letters. Then, they will practice writing words. Last, they will write an animal fact on each page.

The best way to learn writing in cursive is through practice. This book gives your learner so many opportunities to practice without being monotonous. We are confident that they will love the journey to being a great cursive writer.

Happy learning!

Handwriting Before and After

Before starting the book and upon completion, write out the following sentences and see how much you've improved!

Write: This is my cursive before.

Write: This is my cursive after.

Trace and Write Letters

In this section of the book, you will practice writing each letter of the alphabet in cursive. Each page contains a different letter. We will start with capital letters and then practice lowercase letters. Make sure to read the animal fact on the top of each page, too!

For the best results, complete this workbook in order. Take your time and complete every page. Sit in your chair with your feet flat on the ground and under the table. Practice using proper pencil grasp.

Pay attention to the first letter on each page that includes numbers and arrows on the letter. This will show you exactly how you should write the letter and the order of your pencil strokes.

First, you will trace the dotted letters. Then, practice writing your letters on your own. You are on your way to great cursive handwriting.

Happy writing!

Apes learn best by observing others.

Butterflies actually have four
wings, not two.

Cats are a bit color-blind and
can mostly see blue and green.

Ducks can sleep with one eye open
to protect themselves.

 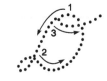 

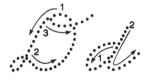 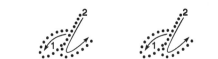

5

Eagles can live for up to thirty years in the wild.

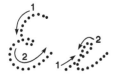

Flamingos build nests out of mud.

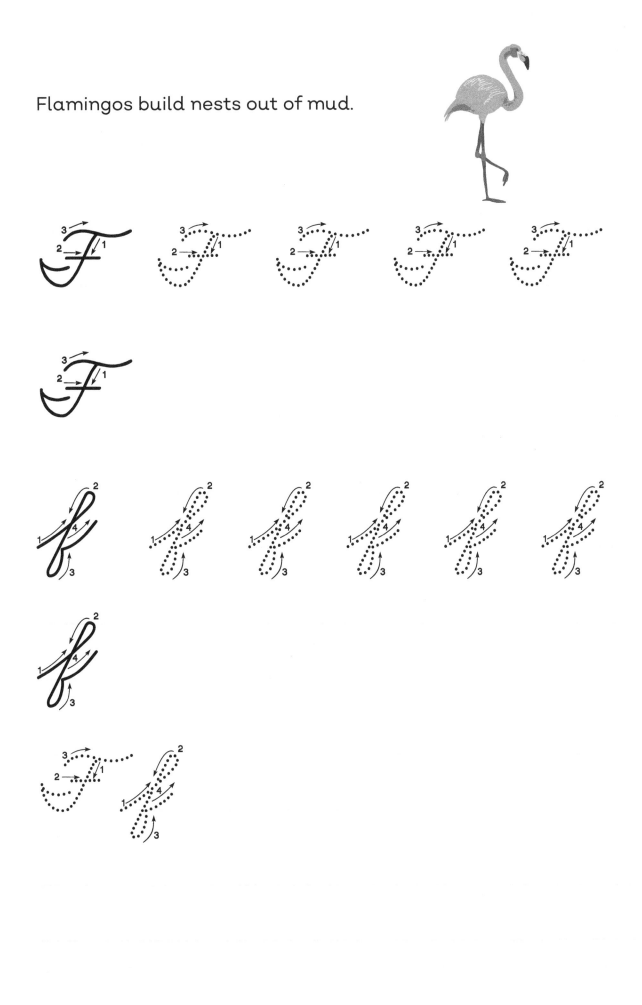

A giraffe's tongue can be
blue, black, or purple.

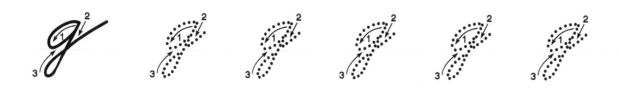

A hippopotamus can weigh up to 3,000 pounds, but they only eat plants.

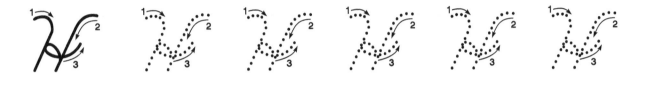

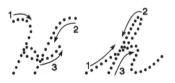

Iguanas have special taste buds
on their tongues to help them smell.

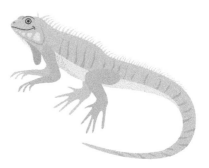

Some jellyfish will glow in the dark
to scare off predators.

 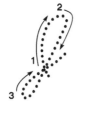 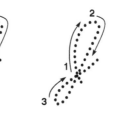

 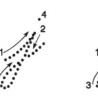

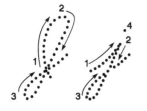

A koala gets most of its water from eucalyptus tree leaves and trunks.

Llamas are very quiet animals
and communicate by humming.

Only female mosquitoes bite humans.

14

Narwhals can hold their breath
for twenty-five minutes.

An ostrich's eye is bigger
than its brain.

16

Pigs roll in the mud to keep
themselves cool.

   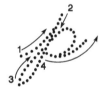

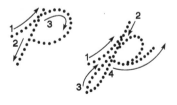

Quaggas are said to have stripes only
on their heads and necks.

A young rooster is called a cockerel.

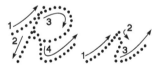

Baby squirrels are blind until
they are five to six weeks old.

Turtles and tortoises have
beaks instead of teeth.

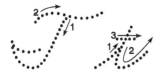

The unau is a two-toed sloth that
sleeps up to twenty hours a day.

Some vultures eat ostrich eggs by
using stones to break the shells.

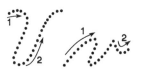

Female walruses are pregnant
for fifteen to sixteen months.
The baby is called a calf.

X-ray tetra are fish with
see-through skin that live in
the Amazon River.

Yellow jackets do not like the smell
of spearmint or peppermint.

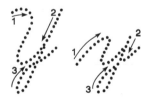

Zebras run in a zigzag pattern
to avoid predators.

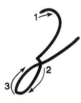

 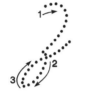 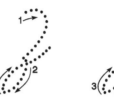 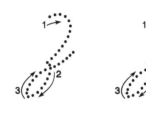

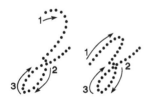

Great work so far! Take a quick break and enjoy coloring this cat.

Trace and Write Words

Way to go! You have practiced writing the entire alphabet in cursive. Now, let's practice writing words. On each page, you will learn to write three different words that can be found in the animal fact at the top of the page.

Trace each word and then write each word on your own. Use the space provided to write each word as many times as you can. If you feel confident, try writing with a pen.

You are doing great!

The tongue of an anteater
can be two feet long.

anteater

feet feet feet feet

long long

A Cape buffalo can tip a car over.

buffalo buffalo

tip tip tip tip

car car car

A donkey loves to eat bananas.

donkey donkey

loves loves

eat eat eat eat

An elephant walks on the tips of its toes.

elephant

walks walks

toes toes toes

A gazelle can jump ten feet high.

gazelle gazelle

jump jump

high high

A hedgehog grunts when
it digs for bugs.

hedgehog

grunts grunts

bugs bugs bugs

A monkey has fingerprints like a human.

monkey

has has has

human

A shark can have 300 teeth
at one time.

shark shark

teeth teeth

time time

A tiger can swim and loves the water.

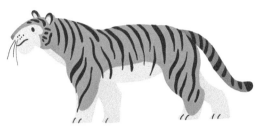

tiger tiger

swim swim

water water

A rabbit keeps itself clean
by licking its own fur.

rabbit rabbit

clean clean

fur fur fur

A lion can sleep for twenty hours a day.

lion lion

sleep sleep sleep

day day day

Only male moose have antlers.

moose moose

have have

antlers antlers

An octopus can eat its own arms.

octopus *octopus*

own *own*

arms *arms*

A panda has six fingers on each paw.

panda panda

six six six six

each each each

A wolf pup is born blind and deaf.

wolf wolf

born born

blind blind

A snake can smell with its tongue.

snake snake

its its its its

tongue tongue

A boar has sharp teeth called tusks.

boar boar

sharp sharp

tusks tusks

A chameleon changes
colors based on its mood.

chameleon

colors colors

mood mood

A badger can dig deep
underground tunnels.

badger badger

dig dig dig

deep deep deep

A snail can hibernate in colder months.

snail snail

hibernate

months

You are doing great! Take a quick break and enjoy coloring these sharks.

Trace and Write
Animal Facts

Great job writing so many words! You should be proud of yourself. Let's keep going by practicing writing sentences.

Throughout this book, you have learned a lot of animal facts. In this section of the book, you will practice tracing and writing more facts about animals. On the first half of the page, read the fact and then trace it. Then, on the second half of the page, write it on your own.

Share the facts with your family or friends. What is your favorite animal fact so far? You are doing great.

Have fun writing!

Baby pigeons
are called
squabs.

Horses breathe
through
their noses.

Toucans hop more than they fly.

A polar bear can swim far without rest.

Deer have hooves on their feet.

Hummingbirds can fly backward.

Crabs use gills to breathe.

Woodpeckers have furry noses.

A clownfish

is covered

with mucus.

Leopards don't need to drink water.

Owls can

fly almost

silently.

Sheep, cows, and goats are related.

A mouse eats
up to twenty
times a day.

A lizard can
detach its
own tail.

Female
reindeer have
antlers, too.

Dogs can tell
when someone
is sick.

Goats know
when you
are happy.

Stingrays
give birth to
live babies.

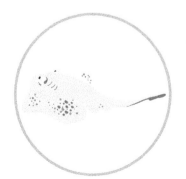

A zebra's skin is black under its stripes.

Lemurs like to sunbathe together.

You should be so proud of your progress. Let's enjoy one last coloring break. Don't forget to go back to the Handwriting Before and After page at the beginning of the book to see how much you've improved!

Certificate of Completion

This certificate is presented to:

for working so hard to improve their cursive handwriting!

Date _____

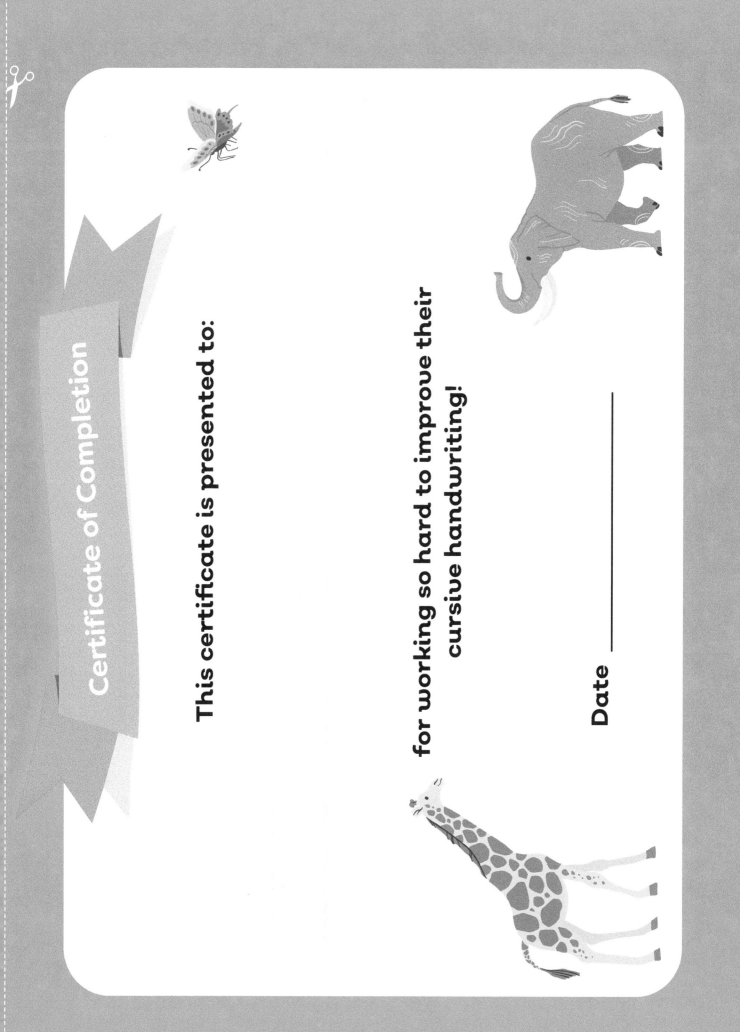

About the Author

CRYSTAL RADKE is a bestselling author, educational leader, and public speaker. After spending time as a kindergarten teacher, she began her consultant business where she mentors early childhood educators by providing inspirational keynotes and powerful professional development. Her degrees in education and experience as a foster and adoptive mother have made helping children learn and grow a personal mission. She writes the website KreativeinKinder.com.